Dear mommy
Happy ranlentines
day
and make it
"Hoppy"

Ribit

Torie

Charlie

What Is a Mother?

The C. R. Gibson Company
Norwalk, Connecticut

Mother—a word that holds the tender spell
Of all the dear essential things of earth;

GRACE NOLL CROWELL

What Is a Mother?

DEFINITION

I search among the plain and lovely words
To find what one word "Mother" means; as well
Try to define the tangled song of birds;
The echo in the hills of one clear bell.
One cannot snare the wind, or catch the wings
Of shadows flying low across the wheat;
Ah, who can prison simple, natural things
That make the long days beautiful and sweet?

Mother—a word that holds the tender spell
Of all the dear essential things of earth;
A home, clean sunlit rooms, and the good smell
Of bread; a table spread; a glowing hearth.
And love beyond the dream of anyone . . .
I search for words for her . . . and there are none.

GRACE NOLL CROWELL

A PRIZE TRIBUTE TO MOTHER

Youngest of a family of seven girls and a boy, younger than most of her classmates, and an honor student, fourteen-year-old Esther Elwofsky achieved a new distinction by putting down in a few simple words all that she feels for her mother.

One day in the year is set aside for mothers—how strange a custom! Like setting one day aside to grasp the beauty of the sun, the moon, the stars—all the lovely, natural things that bring warmth, light, comfort.

Many times I have longed to set my thoughts down upon paper. Not in the flowery language of greeting-cards, but in the simple language of love. I write the words, "Dear Mother"—lovely tender words—and grow silent beneath the weight of thoughts and memories that, lying buried like precious jewels beneath the dust of years, arise clear and glowing in my mind.

Impossible to describe the homely beauty of these thoughts: warm kitchen filled with the scent of bread; sunlight dappling a clean white cloth, touching the rosy apples in their copper bowl; tender memories of loving acts and dreary tasks done smilingly while the sun shone and the years marched swiftly past, and youth, perhaps secretly mourned, passed with it.

How describe the broad, deep-bosomed earth, symbol of maternity—awakening in the spring of the year, lying fruitful beneath the summer sun, resting from its labors in the autumn, and dreaming peacefully wrapt in snowy mantle? Dwelling upon these thoughts we hear, borne strong on the wind, the galloping hoofs of Time astride the ceaseless cycles of the years, drawing nearer and nearer. Then, caught by a vague fear, we say or we think or we write, "Dear Mother."

Oh, the love of a mother,
love which none can forget.

VICTOR HUGO

Everybody knows that a good mother gives her children
a feeling of trust and stability. She is their earth. She is
the one they can count on for the things that matter
most of all. She is their food and their bed and the extra
blanket when it grows cold in the night; she is their
warmth and their health and their shelter, she is the one
they want to be near when they cry. She is the only
person in the whole world or in a whole lifetime who can
be these things to her children. There is no substitute for
her. Somehow even her clothes feel different to her
children's hands from anybody else's clothes. Only to
touch her skirt or her sleeve makes a troubled child feel
better.

KATHERINE BUTLER HATHAWAY

A Mother's Love Is . . .

In afterlife you may have friends, fond, dear friends, but never will you have again the inexpressible love and gentleness lavished upon you, which none but a mother bestows.

THOMAS BABINGTON MACAULAY

A mother's love for the child
of her body differs essentially
from all other affections, and
burns with so steady and clear
a flame that it appears like the
one unchangeable thing in
this earthly mutable life, so that
when she is no longer present
it is still a light to our steps
and a consolation.

W. H. HUDSON

Mother is the name for God in the lips and hearts of little children.

WILLIAM MAKEPEACE THACKERAY

Mother.
"The sweetest name in the English language," my own mother used to say. True, she was a sentimentalist—but surely we have a right to be sentimental when it comes to mothers. The very word *Motherhood* has an emotional depth and significance few terms have. It bespeaks nourishment and safety and sheltering arms. It embraces not only the human state but the animal kingdom—the tiger fiercely protective of her cubs, the hen clucking over her brood and spreading her wings to shield them from the storm. It speaks of the very beginnings of life in egg or womb, and of nurture in the most critical stages thereafter.

MARJORIE HOLMES

Blessed are the mothers of the earth,
for they have combined the practical
and the spiritual into the workable
way of human life. They have darned
little stockings, mended little dresses,
washed little faces, and have pointed
little eyes to the stars and little souls
to eternal things.

WILLIAM L. STIDGER

MOTHER'S SONG

When the voices of children are heard on the green
And laughing is heard on the hill,
My heart is at rest within my breast
   And everything else is still.

'Then come home, my children, the sun is gone down
And the dews of night arise;
Come, come, leave off play, and let us away
Till the morning appears in the skies.'

'No, no, let us play, for it is yet day
And we cannot go to sleep;
Besides in the sky the little birds fly
And the hills are all cover'd with sheep.'

'Well, well, go and play till the light fades away
And then go home to bed.'
The little ones leaped and shouted and laughed
   And all the hills echoed.

WILLIAM BLAKE

Thanks For a Wonderful Childhood

In a loving letter, actress Martha Hyer, who is now primarily on the domestic scene, thanks her mother for warm memories and a devoted upbringing—the gift of love.

Dear Mom,

Whenever I hear about some youngster having problems with his parents—and the fault invariably laid at the parents' door—I can't help but count the blessings of my own childhood. I was lucky. I had you. There were times, I know, when I was a problem to you—but I can't remember ever feeling that the reverse was true.

Your sense of humor touched everything. Your nickname, "The Flea," summed it up: You were tiny and always busy. And so you remained, by any name—Agnes, Mrs. Julien Hyer, Mom,—and the title so many people used for you: great lady. Little wonder that now, when someone says to me, "You're just like your mother," the compliment fills me with pride.

The older I get, the closer I feel to you; the more I understand and appreciate what you were to me; the more grateful I am that you and Pop didn't let us—Aggie, Jean and me—rule the roost. You were "square" enough to have rules and to enforce them; you clung to traditions and taught us to honor, and so to cherish them. You disciplined us only to prepare us for the challenges ahead. You gave us a strong foundation upon which to build our lives.

You were single-minded in the way you reared us. Simply put, your family was everything—and you built your life around us.

Your idea of "liberation" seemed to be the freedom to spend 24 hours a day on your "job." And I don't believe I ever heard you complain. Your beautiful face radiated smiles—the reflection of a generous soul. Some might call a good disposition a gift, but I believe it was your own generosity toward others that was at the core of that rare and wonderful quality you had.

I remember:

Sunday-morning church services. How you stressed the importance of faith in a loving God!

Your pride in our accomplishments, and your compassion when we failed.

Your goodness, kindness, dignity. The ability you had to see beauty and wonder in everything, and to make us see it, too.

Your reassuring presence—ready to help, to forgive, to share, to understand.

I cherish two little cards on which you wrote some thoughts. One reads:

"There is no right way to do a wrong thing."

The other.

"The time to be happy is now,
The place to be happy is here,
The way to be happy is to make others happy.
And make your own heaven right here."

You did this, Mom, for all of us.

YOUR MARTY

THAT'S WHAT MOTHERS ARE FOR

"That's what mothers are for," she said
When thanked for combing a tumbled head,
Or spreading a slice of jelly-bread—
"That's what mothers are for."

"That's what mothers are for," she smiled,
Soothing the sobs of a frightened child,
Ironing a dress from a basket piled—
"That's what mothers are for."

"That's what mothers are for—" Today
When my own children rush in from play
To be mended or cuddled or helped on their way
Her voice echoes as I too say:
"That's what mothers are for!"

MARJORIE HOLMES

PERFECT MOMENT

Somewhere along the road between "beginning" and "ending" there is a perfect moment for every living soul. There may possibly be more than one. But for the most part we are too busy, too young, too adult, too sophisticated, too this or too that to recognize it—and so the moment may be lost.

My perfect moment came when I was eight years old. I awoke one spring night to find moonlight flooding my room through the open window. It was so bright that I sat up in bed. There was no sound at all anywhere. The air was soft and heavy with the fragrance of pear blossoms and honeysuckle.

I crept out of bed and tiptoed softly out of the house. Eight-year-olds were not supposed to be astir at this hour. But I wanted to sit in the swing for a while and watch the moonlight. As I closed the door behind me, I saw my mother sitting on the porch steps. She looked up and smiled and, putting her finger to her lips, reached out with her other hand and drew me down beside her. I sat as close as I could and she put her arm around me.

The whole countryside was hushed and sleeping; no lights burned in any house. The moonlight was liquid silver and so bright we could see the dark outline of the woods a mile away. "Isn't it beautiful?" I whispered, and Mother's arm tightened about me.

Our shepherd dog, Frollo, came across the lawn and stretched himself out contentedly, his head on Mother's lap. For a long time we were all three perfectly still. The stars were pale and far away. Now and then the moonlight would strike a leaf of the Marechal Niel rose beside the porch and be caught for an instant in a dewdrop like a tiny living spark. The shrubs were hung with necklaces of diamonds, and the grass was sweet with dampness.

We knew that in the dark woods there were movement and sound among the wild things—the rabbits and squirrels, the opossums and chipmunks, as they moved about in their own world. And in the shadowy garden, and in the fields, things were growing. In the meadow the foal slept beside its mother, and nearby a young calf nuzzled its mother.

In all this great brooding silence that seemed so infinite, the miracle of life was going on unseen and unheard. The moving of the stars, the planets, the countless worlds, all were governed and held within the safety of the omnipotent yet gentle hand of the Creator.

Mother pointed toward the cedar tree. "Look," she whispered softly, "that star seems caught in the branches."

As we watched it, suddenly from the topmost point of a pear tree a mockingbird burst into song. It was as though the joy that overflowed his heart must find expression. The notes were pure gold, free and clear and liquid as the moonlight, rising, falling, meltingly sweet. At times they were so soft as to be barely audible; then he would sing out, a rapturous profondo. As suddenly as it had begun, the concert ended and the night was silvery still again.

An eight-year-old does not analyze his thoughts, he may not even be aware that he is surrounded by infinity. But he sees a star impaled on the branch of a cedar tree, and knows pure ecstasy. He hears a mockingbird sing in the moonlight, and is filled with speechless joy. He feels his mother's arms about him, and knows complete security.

GLADYS BELL

SONG TO A MOTHER

Bright twinkles in the steady glow of Time
Are vital gifts my mother left with me;
Recalling them evokes a golden chime
Within my memory.
With firm foundation-stones of faith and truth,
She sought to fashion outlooks straight and tall;
Yet fleeting gestures, signs impressed on youth
Are those I best recall:

The scraping of the blade criss-crossed on bread
To bless it ere she sliced the loaf, home-made;
Her flanneled vigil guarding by my bed
When fears or fevers stayed;
The laugh that made duet with mine; the gay
Pure hands that labored on past graying embers;
I hope such tender scenes will be, one day,
The gifts my child remembers.

JEAN CARPENTER MERGARD

Memories

I can still smell the warm spicy smells of gingersnaps
baking in the oven, of apple pies rich with cinnamon,
and of countless doughnuts merrily bobbing about on
the surface of boiling fat. My mother sang hymns as she
went about her work and often encouraged us to sing
with her. One of her favorites was "Shall we gather at
the river?" and all of us, joining in the chorus, loved to
assure her that we would most certainly gather there.
"Yes, we'll gather at the river, the beautiful river, the
beautiful river," we would all shout together, each, I feel
sure, thinking of that river only as some pleasant family
picnicking ground on some pleasant undefined day in
the future.

MARY ELLEN CHASE

MOTHER'S HANDS

I remember she used often to look somewhat ruefully at her hands, those beautiful, useful, roughened hands of hers, so strong in the palm, so unexpectedly delicate and pointed in the fingers; not small hands, but having spare and well-shaped lines. It was always her plan that one day she would stop plunging her hands into this and that; she was going to wear gloves when she gardened and use cold cream and have really "nice" hands.

My memory of her is of someone always marvelously fresh and pretty, although when I examine it I see that she wore the same dresses year after year. But she could twist a ribbon in such a way or so pin a flower at her throat that she looked as though she wore a new gown. There was that air about her. I remember that she had a large old tin box in the attic where she put every hat, I believe, she ever owned, when it grew past use, and every flower of silk or bit of ribbon. Twice a year she cried gaily, "We must go to Paris to buy our hats for the season!"

And with great ceremony we went to the attic and opened the tin box and out of it by means of her skillful fingers hats were made for herself and the two girls. If anything her hats were prettier than any I saw elsewhere, and had style. At any rate, her imagination and gay nonsense and swift fingers created for us all the illusion and excitement of shopping for a new hat. Years later when I really did go to Paris to buy a new hat there was not half the edge of excitement in it that there had been in the old expeditions up the attic stairs to Paris in a tin box.

PEARL S. BUCK

MEMORIES

Tucked away in the memories of my childhood
*   Is the smile of a loving face,*
A gentle hand that led me—
*   No other could fill its place.*

When childish woes oppressed me,
*   And I was filled with terrors and tears,*
That loving hand caressed me
*   While she shared the wisdom of years.*

Now years have grown upon me—
*   Both joy and sorrow I have known;*
But the memory always lingers
*   Of that wonderful Mother at home.*

MARY BOND WEBER

DAYS WHEN I AM SEWING

A thousand things remind us of our mothers—
But days when I am sewing you return
Most easily: in the mystery of laying
A tissue pattern out to best advantage,
In the scissors' clean bite of the crispy goods,
The basting (thank you for insisting on it),
The stitching, and the ultimate delight
Of seeing garments grow to perfect fit.

Some mothers come back best in poetry
Or music, or good laughter, or in gardens—
But, days when I am sewing, I admit
I never can be certain whether my
Hands happily repeat the tricks you taught,
Or these are your hands, come alive in me.

ELAINE V. EMANS

WOMAN AT WINDOW

No volition sent her toward the window.
Indeed, she never knew
That she was standing there and staring.
Till something brought her to.

Then, with a pang, she suddenly remembered
How her mother used to be:
So often, hand to cheek, and staring, staring
At things she *didn't see.*

DOROTHY ALDIS

There never was a woman like her. She was gentle as a dove and brave as a lioness . . . The memory of my mother and her teachings were after all the only capital I had to start life with, and on that capital I have made my way.

ANDREW JACKSON

A wise mother reminds her child of the sheer joy of living.

THE DAY WE FLEW THE KITES

"String!" shouted Brother, bursting into the kitchen. "We need lots more string."

It was Saturday. As always, it was a busy one, for "Six days shalt thou labor and do all thy work" was taken seriously then. Outside, Father and Mr. Patrick next door were doing chores.

Inside the two houses, Mother and Mrs. Patrick were engaged in spring cleaning. Such a windy March day was ideal for "turning out" clothes closets. Already woolens flapped on back-yard clotheslines.

Somehow the boys had slipped away to the back lot with their kites. Now, even at the risk of having Brother impounded to beat carpets, they had sent him for more string. Apparently there was no limit to the heights to which kites would soar today.

My mother looked out the window. The sky was piercingly blue; the breeze fresh and exciting. Up in all that blueness sailed puffy billows of clouds. It had been a long, hard winter, but today was Spring.

Mother looked at the sitting room, its furniture disordered for a Spartan sweeping. Again her eyes wavered toward the window. "Come on, girls! Let's take string to the boys and watch them fly the kites a minute." On the way we met Mrs. Patrick, laughing guiltily, escorted by her girls.

There never was such a day for flying kites! God doesn't make two such days in a century. We played all our fresh twine into the boys' kites and still they soared. We could hardly distinguish the tiny, orange-colored specks. Now and then we slowly reeled one in, finally bringing it dipping and tugging to earth, for the sheer joy of sending it up again. What a thrill to run with them, to the right, to the left, and see our poor, earthbound movements reflected minutes later in the majestic sky-dance of the kites! We wrote wishes on slips of paper and slipped them over the string. Slowly, irresistibly, they climbed up until they reached the kites. Surely all such wishes would be granted!

Even our fathers dropped hoe and hammer and joined us. Our mothers took their turn, laughing like schoolgirls. Their hair blew out of their pompadours and curled loose about their cheeks; their gingham aprons whipped about their legs. Mingled with our fun was something akin to awe. The grownups were really playing with us! Once I looked at Mother and thought she looked actually pretty. And her over forty!

We never knew where the hours went on that hilltop day. There were no hours, just a golden, breezy Now. I think we were all a little beyond ourselves. Parents forgot their duty and their dignity; children forgot their combativeness and small spites. "Perhaps it's like this in the Kingdom of Heaven," I thought confusedly.

It was growing dark before, drunk with sun and air, we all stumbled sleepily back to the houses. I suppose we had some sort of supper. I suppose there must have been a surface tidying-up, for the house on Sunday looked decorous enough.

The strange thing was, we didn't mention that day afterward. I felt a little embarrassed. Surely none of the others had thrilled to it as deeply as I. I locked the memory up in that deepest part of me where we keep "the things that cannot be and yet are."

The years went on, then one day I was scurrying about my own kitchen in a city apartment, trying to get some work out of the way while my three-year-old insistently cried her desire to "go park and see ducks."

"I *can't* go!" I said. "I have this and this to do, and when I'm through I'll be too tired to walk that far."

My mother, who was visiting us, looked up from the peas she was shelling. "It's a wonderful day," she offered; "really warm, yet there's a fine, fresh breeze. It reminds me of that day we flew the kites."

I stopped in my dash between stove and sink. The locked door flew open, and with it a gush of memories. I pulled off my apron. "Come on," I told my little girl. "You're right, it's too good a day to miss."

FRANCES FOWLER

AT THE END OF THE DAY

My desk is always littered
With things I want to keep;
They should be cleared away
Before I go to sleep.

Announcements of events gone by
To tell of death or birth,
A greeting from a distant friend;
These really have no worth.

A picture of a romping pup,
A withered wedding rose,
A daughter's little copy book;
I've many more of those.

A husband's useless, loving gift,
A small son's trial at art;
Of no value to the hand or mind,
Their merit's in the heart.

My life is always baffled
By things I want to do;
They cannot be attained
Before my life is through.

My mind would steer a steady course
Directly toward the goal;
My heart stops at so many ports
For cargo for the soul.

IOWA MARSHALL MAPLETHORPE

They Write of Mothers

CORSAGE

Mother, Mother,
The florist's boy knocks,
With his hat in his hand
And a great green box.

Hurry, lift the cover;
See, untie the bow . . .
Four pink camellias
Fastened in a row.

Mother, mother,
Please, and shut your eyes!
This *is from me.*
This is a surprise.

Yellow dandelions
With tangly silk hair. . . .
Mother, mother,
Which shall you wear?

ETHEL JACOBSON

Mother—that was the bank where we deposited all our hurts and worries.

DE WITT TALMAGE

MY MOTHER

My mother's love is larkspur, blue and sweet,
The gentle wind along a quiet street.
My mother's love is little silver singing
Of twilight bells, the soft and soundless winging
Of birds in flight across an evening sky,
The first star, gold and high;
And on all pathways, whether joy or grief,
The clear, unwavering candle of belief.

GRACE V. WATKINS

The woman who creates and sustains a home, and under
whose hands children grow up to be strong and pure
men and women is a creator second only to God.

HELEN HUNT JACKSON

THEY WRITE OF MOTHERS. . . .

They write of mothers with snowy hair,
And faces old and wrinkled,
And gentle, folded, careworn hands
That oft with tears are sprinkled.
I wish some one would write a song
For mothers young and gay,
With well-kept hair and skin and hands
And tears they've dashed away.

MARION BEARD

TO MY MOTHER

"When I grow up", I had always said,
Squaring my shoulders and shaking my head,
"I'll do whatever I want to do. . . . "
But I always came back for a kiss from you.
When I grew up I was somewhat stern
And wondered if you would ever learn
That I was adult and therefore wise
But I leaned on the love in your steady eyes.
With what true thread of wisdom and dream
You mended the sails and stitched the seam
Of my wayward craft, I cannot know;
I can only write as the swift years go
With the tides of time, we have shared together
A lovely mother-and-daughter weather
And kept in balance a sweet and fine
Ebb and flow of your heart and mine.

GLADYS McKEE

MY WILD IRISH MOTHER

Jean Kerr, eminently successful mother, playwright and author, introduces us to her very special, high-spirited, energetic Irish mother.

I'm never going to write my autobiography *and it's all my mother's fault.* I didn't hate her, so I have practically no material. In fact, the situation is worse than I'm pretending. We were crazy about her—and you know I'll never get a book out of that, much less a musical.

Mother was born Kitty O'Neill, in Kinsale, Ireland, with bright red hair, bright blue eyes, and the firm conviction that it was wrong to wait for an elevator if you were only going up to the fifth floor. . . .

. . . To the four low-metabolism types she inexplicably produced, Mother's energy has always seemed awesome. "What do you think," she's prone to say, "do I have time to cut the grass before I stuff the turkey?" But her whirlwind activity is potentially less dangerous than her occasional moments of repose. Then she sits, staring into space, clearly lost in languorous memories. The faint, fugitive smile that hovers about her lips suggests the gentle melancholy of one hearing Mozart played beautifully. Suddenly she leaps to her feet. "I know it will work," she says. "All we have to do is remove that wall, plug up the windows, and extend the porch."

It's undoubtedly fortunate that she has the thrust and the energy of a well-guided missile. Otherwise she wouldn't get a lick of work done, because everybody who comes to her house, stays at least an hour. I used to think that they were one and all beguiled by her Irish accent. But I have gradually gleaned that they are telling her the story of their invariably unhappy lives. Mother's credo, by the way, is that if you want something, anything, don't just sit there—pray for it. And she combines a Job-like patience in the face of the mysterious ways of the Almighty with a flash of Irish rebellion which will bring her to say—and I'm sure she speaks for many of us—"Jean, what I am really looking for is a blessing that's *not* in disguise."

She does have a knack for penetrating disguises, whether it be small boys who claim that they have taken baths or middle-aged daughters who swear that they have lost five pounds. Some time ago I had a collection of short pieces brought out in book form and I sent one of the first copies to Mother. She was naturally delighted. Her enthusiasm fairly bubbled off the pages of the letter. "Darling," she wrote, "isn't it marvelous the way those old pieces of yours finally came to the surface like a dead body!"

I knew when I started this that all I could do was list the things Mother says, because it's not possible, really, to describe her.

However, I recognize, if I cannot describe, the lovely festive air she always brings with her, so that she can arrive any old day in July and suddenly it seems to be Christmas Eve and the children seem handsomer and better behaved and all the adults seem more charming and—

Well, you'll just have to meet her.

A mother's heart is always with her children.

GERMAN PROVERB

Some are kissing mothers and
some are scolding mothers,
but it is love just the same,
and most mothers kiss and
scold together.

PEARL S. BUCK

The mother-child relationship
is paradoxical and, in a sense,
tragic. It requires the most
intense love on the mother's
side, yet this very love must
help the child grow away from
the mother, and to become
fully independent.

ERICH FROMM

Be as unsentimental about it as you wish, there is still no
denying that the homemaker moves in the honorable
tradition of the makers and molders of society. Here you
are and here is the plastic clay. And when you have done
with it what you will, here after all is the pivot center of
the world.

PHILIP WYLIE

Home Means Mother

MOTHERS

Mothers choose lovely, simple things
When they would make a home,
Fires on a hearth, a kettle's song,
Lamps for the feet that roam,
Chant of a lullaby in the dusk,
Cookie jars on low shelves,
Prayers that are coined with rhyming words,
Stories of kings and elves,

Cakes where the birthday candles shine,
Secrets that child-lips speak,
Brief wounds that need a healing touch,
Marbles and hide-and-seek—
Mothers give up their hearts' deep dreams.
But women can understand
That there is a compensating joy
In the clasp of a small child's hand.

HELEN WELSHIMER

DAY'S END

Our living room at evening takes on a mongrel air,
Without a sign of pedigree or mark of morning care.

Exactitude has perished beneath the evening feet
And disarray has entered with vigor from the street.

Its lampshades angle strangely; its curtains seem
  awry;
And yet it cocks a friendly ear and blinks a peace-
  ful eye.

It wags indeed a livelier tail, the voice too big,
  perhaps.
Yet wholesomer, I will admit, than soft, anemic
  yaps.

Papa and paper fill one chair, daughter and dolls,
  the floor.
Son and sounds are going the rounds, which Mama
  must ignore.

And cozily at bedtime, unmindful of its flaws,
It slumbers as it pleases with litter round its
  paws.

ISABELLE BRYANS LONGFELLOW

The Bible does not say very much about homes; it says a great deal about the things that make them. It speaks about life and love and joy and peace and rest! If we get a house and put these into it, we shall have secured a home.

JOHN HENRY JOWETT

WHAT IS A FAMILY?

A family is a single word—
in the heart heard—
meaning beyond its syllables,
its hyphen ties of mother-son,
father-daughter, miracles
of loyalty and communion.

Say it and any heart grows firm!
It is a contract, it is a term
of time that compasses the past
and finds and makes the future fast—
a knee to sit on, a head to pat—
and a natural habitat!

In all you have tried to do, or planned
it must stand behind you, or offer cheer,
or hope a little, or lend a hand.
Courage! it cries, There is someone here!

HELEN HARRINGTON

LITANY FOR CHILDREN'S DAY

We have dedicated this day to our children;

> And for our children on this day,
> We dream great dreams of their tomorrows.

Let this be our dream for our children:
That they may always know,
In the brief and fleeting years of childhood,
The warmth of our unfailing love—

> For only thus shall they learn to love.

Let this be our dream for our children:
That they may always find us, their elders,
Seeking to preserve and to create things of enduring
    beauty—

> For only thus shall they learn to love the beau-
>   tiful, and to live beautifully.

Let this be our dream for our children:

That they may ever find us, their elders,
Open and receptive to new truths,
And eager in the quest for knowledge—

For only thus shall they become lovers of and
  seekers after truth.

Humbly, hopefully, devotedly,
We dream these dreams for our children:

  And may ours be the sobering knowledge
  That only through *our deeds*
  Can all these dreams come true.
            Amen

                              WILLIAM D. HAMMOND

  Many of the strongest influences
  for nobility in living come to us
  through the precepts our mothers
  taught us, or through the examples
  they set for us as they moved
  about as the queens of their homes
  and the inspirers of our deepest love.

                              LEO BENNETT

A TOAST

Whene'er you find a happy home,
With smiling faces in it,
Where loving hearts and busy hands
Are speeding every minute;

Where every one is quite content,
With one thing or another,
You'll know there lies within that home,
A wise and loving mother.

ANONYMOUS

JUST TO BE NEEDED

"She always seems so tied" is what friends say;
She never has a chance to get away.
Home, husband, children, duties great or small,
Keep her forever at their beck and call.
But she confides, with laughter in her eyes,
She never yet felt fretted by these ties.
"Just to be needed is more sweet," says she,
"Than any freedom in this world could be."

MARY EVERSLEY

MOTHER

To be a mother is the greatest
vocation in the world. No being
has a position of such great power
and influence. She holds in her
hands the destiny of nations; for
to her is necessarily committed the
making of the nation's citizens.

HANNAH WHITALL SMITH

AWARENESS

One of life's major tragedies, both for parents and for children, lies in the fact that the joys of today are all about us, unrecognized. Obviously, a father would defeat his purpose (and be a bore) if he studded the family conversation with rhapsodic exclamations, "What a good time I'm having shining my shoes! The rhythm of the brush! The redolence of the shoe cream! The highlights that the sunshine makes upon the polished leather!" Likewise a mother would kill the thing she tries to foster if she went about exclaiming, "Ah me! the silver egg-beater in a yellow bowl whipping thick white cream! What color! What texture! What beauty!" And yet it is just such unexpected homely incidents which make the sensitive individual catch his breath with wonder for the manifold beauties of everyday life; sunshine edging the drawn window shade and falling slantwise across a dark rug; a child bouncing upstairs with her own joyous rhythm; dandelions rioting in a vacant lot; rusty grasses along the roadside—these and a thousand other wonders crowding the most commonplace day.

Awareness, or learning to live as one goes, is distinctly a habit. A parent may have to cultivate the habit in himself before he can cultivate it in his children. But once awareness becomes a habit, then the spirit rushes forth with ecstasy to moments of aliveness it would otherwise have missed—and never know how great was its poverty in the missing.

MARGUERITTE HARMON BRO

FIRST MOTHER

The Lord God walked in the morning cool
When the earth was a new green ball,
And He said: I shall make her beautiful
This woman to watch over all.

The brooding strength of the hills he bound
To the budding girth of a tree,
And into the golden dust of the ground
He breathed bright ecstasy.

And the woman walked in the morning cool
A heartless thing and vain;
And the Lord God said: She is beautiful,
But she lacks the grace of pain.

Then a moaning forced her lips apart,
While ministering angels smiled,
And into her body came a heart,
And into her arms a child.

VIVIEN YEISER LARAMORE

ACKNOWLEDGMENTS

The editor and the publisher have made every effort to trace the ownership of all copyrighted material and to secure permission from copyright holders of such material. In the event of any question arising as to the use of any material the publisher and editor, while expressing regret for inadvertent error, will be pleased to make the necessary corrections in future printings. Thanks are due to the following authors, publishers, publications and agents for permission to use the material indicated.

AMERICAN BOOK COMPANY, for "At the End of the Day" by Iowa M. Maplethorpe.

THE CHRISTIAN SCIENCE MONITOR, for "What Is a Family?" by Helen Harrington, copyright © 1961 by The Christian Science Publishing Society.

THOMAS Y. CROWELL COMPANY, INC., for "Mother's Hands" from *The Exile* by Pearl S. Buck, copyright 1936 by Pearl S. Buck. Published by *The John Day Company.*

DOUBLEDAY & COMPANY, INC., for excerpts from *As Tall As My Heart* by Marjorie Holmes, copyright © 1974 by Marjorie Holmes Mighell; for excerpt from "My Wild Irish Mother" by Jean Kerr, copyright © 1960 by The McCall Corporation, from *The Snake Has All the Lines* by Jean Kerr.

ELAINE V. EMANS, for "Days When I Am Sewing."

HARPER & ROW, PUBLISHERS, INC., for "Definition" from *Poems of Inspiration and Courage* by Grace Noll Crowell, copyright 1936 by Harper & Row, Publishers, Inc., renewed 1964 by Grace Noll Crowell.

GLADYS McKEE IKER, for "To My Mother," from the May 1973 issue of *Good Housekeeping* copyright © 1973 by The Hearst Corporation.

BERTHA KLAUSNER INTERNATIONAL LITERARY AGENCY, INC., for excerpt from "When Children Ask" by Marguerite Harmon Bro.

ISABELLE BYRANS LONGFELLOW, for "Day's End," from the May, 1940, issue of *Good Housekeeping* copyright © 1940 by The Hearst Corporation.

MERCHANTS NATIONAL BANK & TRUST COMPANY OF FARGO, for "My Mother" by Grace V. Watkins.

PARENTS' MAGAZINE for "The Day We Flew the Kites" by Frances Fowler, from the May 1949 issue of *Parents' Magazine,* reprinted with permission from the July 1949 *Reader's Digest.*

MILDRED WELSHIMER PHILLIPS, for "Mothers" by Helen Welshimer.

READER'S DIGEST, for "Perfect Moment" by Gladys Bell from the May 1957 issue, copyright © 1957 by The Reader's Digest Association, Inc.

Type set in Corolla

Designed by Thomas James Aaron

Selected by Priscilla Shepard

PHOTO CREDITS